CLOSING THE DEAL

The Power of Relationships in Sales

LEGEND IRA

Closing the deal

Closing the deal

Review

"The Power of Relationships in Sales" is an enthralling examination of the critical role that interpersonal relationships play in the realm of sales. LEGEND IRA brings to fore the art of creating and cultivating connections with customers and clients in this enlightening book on sales relationship, demonstrating how these bonds can be the driving force behind successful sales attempts. This book explains the keys to building long-term relationships with potential clients by using real-world examples, tried-and-true tactics, and expert insights. Readers will discover how to build trust, stay real, and use the strength of relationships to not only make sales but also achieve long-term loyalty and repeat business. "Closing the Deal" provides useful information and practical recommendations that can help you alter your sales strategy, whether

Closing the deal

you're a seasoned sales professional or just starting out. With this must-read book, you'll discover the significant influence that excellent connections can have on your sales career and unleash the real potential of your selling talents.

Introduction

The terrain is continuously changing in the dynamic and competitive world of sales. New technologies are being developed, markets are shifting, and consumer behavior is changing. Despite these changes, one constant remains: connections matter. The capacity to connect with people on a human level is the cornerstone of success, whether you're selling a product, a service, or an idea. "Closing the Deal: The Power of Relationships in Sales" takes you inside the mind of a successful salesperson. This book is your guide to mastering the art of relationship selling, whether you're a seasoned sales professional trying to fine-tune your approach or a beginner eager to learn the tricks of the trade. Why should you be concerned about relationships in sales? Because they serve as a bridge between your products and the requirements, wants, and goals of your customers. We'll look at the principles of relationship selling in this book, providing practical ideas and tactics that you can use right now to develop trust, generate value, and, eventually, complete the purchase. You'll receive a complete grasp of how to utilize connections to reach your sales goals, from the effect of technology and social media to the timeless skill of active listening.

The future of sales belongs to individuals who recognize that it is about more than simply transacting. By the end of this book, you'll have the knowledge and abilities to establish these relationships and propel your sales career to new heights. So, let us move into "Closing the Deal: The Power of Relationships in Sales." Prepare to discover the methods, insights, and tales that will enable you to build lasting relationships, outperform your sales objectives, and write your own sales success story.

key point 1

Creating Stable Foundations

Success in sales is founded on a solid foundation of connections. The first step of our trip will focus on setting the basis for effective relationship selling. Just as a good foundation is required for a durable structure to endure the test of time, your sales efforts rely on developing trust, knowing your audience, and encouraging authenticity from the outset. You must communicate with your clients in a clear, frequent, and polite manner, using the channels and techniques they choose. You must also actively listen, ask pertinent questions, and give feedback and updates. Communication may assist you in avoiding misunderstandings, managing expectations, and resolving problems.

Relationship Selling Fundamentals

Building a functioning connection with consumers is critical to a company's long-term success. A solid relationship built on trust and communication makes customers feel more comfortable and connected to a company, which may lead to increased customer retention and repeat buy rates. To engage on a personal level with potential consumers, sales professionals must have exceptional interpersonal skills. Building trust and understanding consumer demands requires active listening, empathy, and effective communication. Salespeople may build long-term relationships and position themselves as trusted consultants by making real connections. Sales is more than simply closing deals; it is also about developing long-term connections with clients. This pillar highlights the need to provide great customer service even after the deal has been completed. To guarantee client satisfaction, sales professionals should cultivate existing connections, give continuing assistance, and aggressively seek feedback. Customers who are satisfied are more likely to become devoted advocates, make referrals, and contribute to the salesperson's overall success. Getting your potential consumers' attention and trust is an important part of making a transaction. When you build a solid connection with someone, you get their respect, willingness to value your thoughts, and the possibility of long-term business. But the question is, how can you effectively develop rapport?

Understanding Your Target Market

To develop meaningful connections or rapport, you must first understand the people with whom you want to connect. This is all about learning and understanding your target audience. Your target audience is the precise set of consumers that are most likely to need your product or service, and hence the ones who should see your advertising efforts. Age, gender, wealth, geography, hobbies, and a variety of other criteria can all influence the target audience. The consumer controls the purchasing process, and salespeople must build a focused and tailored experiences for prospective clients if they want to stand out against a sea of brands and advertisements. A salesperson may make better-educated judgments about media, messaging, and timing when he has a thorough grasp of his target buyers. A healthy pipeline of qualified leads is critical for sustainable sales growth, according to successful sales professionals. Prospecting is the process of discovering and targeting possible clients who will benefit from the product or service being offered. This may be accomplished through a variety of means, including networking, referrals, cold calling, social media prospecting, and attendance at industry events. Prospecting effectively assures a steady supply of opportunities and raises the likelihood of closing deals.

Creating Trust from the Beginning

Any effective partnership is built on trust. Trust is a currency that delivers long-term dividends. If potential consumers and clients trust you, you're more likely to have a more fruitful interaction with them, which may lead to your customer choosing your services or business. According to a recent HubSpot poll, only 3% of prospects trust sales professionals. Furthermore, 55% of customers do not trust firms as much as they used to. But why is there such a lack of confidence in salespeople? For some, the sales professional has a negative reputation as a result of previous customer experiences with pushiness or dishonesty from the sales rep. You are your first sale! Before a potential consumer buys from you, they must believe that you are looking out for their best interests. Even (and particularly) when selling remotely, you must establish rapport by tailoring your communication style to that of your potential consumer. Understanding their goals and requirements allows you to break through their natural psychological boundaries. At that moment, you'll start to build trust in the connection. Based on that concept, a prospect can only open up to you about their concerns and wants if they trust you. As a result, trust is vital in business since it helps the salesperson understand the client's requirements and aspirations, which helps resolve sales obstacles and leads to more effective selling. Many individuals are now working remotely, either permanently or shortly, and face-to-face exchanges are now screen-to-screen. This applies to both buyers and sellers. What hasn't changed in the sales process is the importance of trust-based partnerships. Trust is the foundation of all strong relationships, whether personal or professional. Indeed, 73% of respondents in a Dale Carnegie survey said trust is "very" essential to them when it comes to creating connections with salespeople. The same survey indicated that 71% of respondents would prefer to buy from a salesperson they trusted than one who provided them the lowest price, demonstrating the essential role trust plays in a buyer-seller relationship. So, just what is trust? In sales, trust is ultimately determined by the customer's view of the salesperson's trustworthiness and if the salesperson is operating in their best interests. While today's distant world in the post-COVID-19 age needs more focus and care to lay the groundwork for a stable, trusted connection, the effort is undoubtedly worthwhile. Buyers are striving to reduce risk in their transactions now more than ever, and this is where trust comes into play. Here are three reasons why trust is important in promoting profitable sales, as supported by further study findings:

- Repeat business is one of the most important long-term effects of a trusted, professional relationship between a buyer and a seller. Most customers would buy from a firm represented by a salesman they trust again.

- Humans are not flawless, and trust leads to rehabilitation. Regardless of how hard a salesman works or how excellent their intentions are, there will be occasions when the consumer is disappointed. The good news is that when consumers trust you, they are more inclined to forgive a mistake or a terrible experience. Customers who trust their salesperson are three times more inclined to overlook a single negative encounter. Customers who trust their salespeople may offer that competitive advantage through their comments at a time when staying ahead of the competition is critical. If they trust their salesperson, the vast majority of customers would be somewhat or very likely to communicate a problem or complaint. The value is in the fact that the customer is not lost at this point. There is still a possibility to recover the client since they are prepared to communicate their issues with the salesperson they trust.

- Trust motivates loyal relationships; the influence of trust may be seen in both consumer attitudes and behaviors that benefit the seller. A devoted, trustworthy consumer, for example, is more likely to share favorable word of mouth. Most clients who trust their salesperson will suggest family or friends and are quite likely to give a favorable review about the salesperson. Trust is your most effective selling weapon; it drives repeat business, recovery, and long-term committed connections. While clients are still price-conscious, a great business connection founded on trust regularly adds to long-term behaviors and emotional attitudes that lead to lucrative sales.

Key idea 2

Relationship Care and Development

After laying a firm basis for relationships, we will now turn our attention to the critical work of sustaining and expanding those connections. Just like a seed takes care and attention to grow into a strong plant, your customer relationships require continual nurturing to develop and yield fruit. We will focus on developing the skills and methods required to cultivate meaningful and long-lasting connections that result in successful sales and return sales.

Strategies for Effective Communication

Almost all connections depend on effective communication. Customers gain trust and respect when they believe they are being heard and understood. Effective communication aids in the development of understanding between you and the customer, which leads to improved engagement and more successful sales. Every effective salesperson understands the importance of communication. Effective communication

Closing the deal

skills are vital for sales success, whether it's understanding client needs, creating relationships, or closing a deal swiftly. Being able to communicate effectively with clients and colleagues may help you create connections, recognize customer requirements, and complete sales faster. Salespeople must have great communication skills to build solid customer connections, engage potential customers, and negotiate the best deal for all parties involved. Strong communication skills may help you better grasp the customer's goals and requirements, allowing you to deliver a customized solution to their problem (and salespeople, after all, are problem solvers). Effective communication aids in the development of understanding between you and the customer, which leads to improved engagement and more successful sales. Strong communication abilities are required to close agreements more quickly. Good communication involves not just understanding the customer's requirements and desires, but also properly explaining the benefits and value of your product or service. You can steer the conversation toward the proper solution if you can successfully connect with potential buyers. Good communication skills are also advantageous throughout the bargaining phase. To properly negotiate a contract, both parties engaged in the sale must communicate effectively. A good negotiation requires both sides to reach an agreement on a mutually beneficial solution. Good communicators can discover areas of agreement quickly, locate common ground, and ensure that everyone's interests are met. This results in speedier transactions and happy clients. Strong communication skills also aid in the rapid development of customer connections. Building connections requires time and trust, but having effective communication skills may considerably speed up the process. Customers who feel understood and appreciated are more likely to purchase from you since they will feel more at ease interacting with you in the future. Building relationships rapidly through excellent communication allows you to close transactions faster while ensuring your consumers remain devoted brand followers. Overall, great communication skills are priceless when it comes to accelerating sales and completing agreements. Understanding consumer demands and being able to successfully explain why your product or service is a good fit for them may assist in persuading potential customers that it is worthwhile to invest in. Negotiating with clarity on both sides guarantees fair conditions for all parties involved, resulting in more effective sales outcomes. Finally, creating relationships rapidly through good communication aids in the closing of sales while maintaining loyal clients in the long run.

Active Listening Techniques

Listening is a quality that is frequently undervalued in sales. Active listening not only fosters trust but also helps you to personalize your solutions to perfectly match the needs of your customers. Be a good listener. Active listening is giving complete attention to the client, understanding and determining their needs and desires. This includes not only hearing what people say but also meditating on their words to ensure you grasp what they mean. This assists salespeople in understanding what the customer needs and to satisfy them with a customized solution that meets their demands.

Managing Customer Expectations

Unmet expectations may be a source of contention in any relationship. Businesses must create clear expectations, communicate effectively, be open, and set expectations along the customer experience to successfully manage expectations. You may send your message through several communication methods while also allowing your customer's voice to be heard. Managing customer expectations is the process of explaining the kind of measures a company may take to accommodate their clients. Setting expectations or boundaries that define the bounds of the business, how far it may go to settle an issue, and when "no" means "no" is also known as setting expectations or boundaries. The key to managing expectations is understanding how far to go to satisfy a customer's need for contentment with their purchase. Businesses exist to provide services and commodities to clients, but they also exist to make a profit to continue to exist. It's a fine line between managing expectations to keeping clients content and returning in the future and the client's unrealistic expectation that a corporation should lose money to keep customers happy. Customers form their own high expectations of what a company should give in terms of customer service. This happens when a company isn't clear about how far it's willing to go to match these unwritten consumer expectations. A company must prevent unpleasant contact with clients, but this is not always attainable. That's why it's critical to set clear expectations about what your company will do to meet a customer's demands while keeping an eye on the wider picture. Continue reading to discover more about the necessity of setting personal standards, how clients build their expectations, and why you must educate your personnel on the art of clearly and gently explaining the customer service guidelines.

Key idea 3

Using Relationships to Increase Sales

How many clients and prospects do you have? Consider your response before responding. Consider all of your current and previous clients and prospects (those old names in your CRM), everyone you've ever met at an industry conference or networking event, everyone you've linked with on LinkedIn, and so on. I'm sure if you add them all up, it's a very remarkable total. Hundreds? Perhaps a few thousand? That's fantastic! So, what do you plan to do with all of those relationships?' Remember, a prospective customer will not buy from you unless they "know you, like you, and trust you." The good news is that those hundreds of existing contacts already know, like, and maybe trust you. So, why not make use of all of those connections? Instead of concentrating your business development efforts on seeking new prospects and clients, make leveraging existing connections the cornerstone of revenue growth. Working with current clients and prospects is quicker, simpler, and less expensive than beginning from scratch. Best wishes!

Changing Prospects into Loyal Customers

The ultimate objective of relationship selling is to convert leads into loyal clients. Not all contacts will become clients, but many will assist you in selling to others by acting as a 'proof source.' Something that "proves you can accomplish what you say you can" is a proof source. Nothing is more appealing to prospective purchasers than evidence that you have done outstanding work for firms comparable to theirs. We all want recommendations, but the vast majority of us wait for them to come to us. Why is this the case? Why not contact current and previous clients and ask for referrals? The same is true for references: contact current and previous clients and ask them to serve as references.

Don't wait for a delighted client to mention anything pleasant about your exceptional job;

instead, ask for it. ("Thank you for your nice remarks, Sam... would you mind putting it in writing?") Also, be certain that they provide you permission to utilize their remarks in your marketing.

Your case studies are your best examples. These are some of the most effective proof sources, but make sure your customer is okay with you exposing some of the specifics of your collaboration. Otherwise, you'll have to make the case study "anonymous."

To make new contacts your old must hear from you first before you can begin to leverage on your ties with them. They need to be reminded that your company exists and can help them. There are two ways to accomplish this:

- Telephone calls. When was the last time you spoke with some of your CRM's older contacts? Make it a habit to pick up the phone and call them. Set aside an hour or two every week (same day, same time) to make it a habit. These calls might help you reconnect with old contacts and even renew a professional relationship. At worst, it's a chance to update your CRM with up-to-date information. There's no way to call the hundreds of contacts in your CRM consistently, so keep them top-of-mind with a monthly e-newsletter. Share informative articles, make downloadable information available, and so forth. Your email platform will be able to tell you who clicked on which link in the email, allowing you to contact them depending on their preferences.

- Revenue increase. Your current clientele already know you, like you, and believe in you. More importantly, they have already begun to spend money on your business. And there is no greater current client than a future client. Look for ways to upsell and cross-sell them... Not only to boost income but because there is a true need. Upselling is the practice of selling upgrades, add-ons, or a wider project scope to raise the amount of the transaction. This referred as the "Would you prefer fries with that?" tactic. A customer, for example, may want their project to be regional whereas the same project at the national level will yield superior results. Cross-selling is the practice of offering additional items and services to a current customer. A research buyer, for example, may engage a research supplier for the qualitative element of a project...However, they may also be a client of that supplier's quantitative services.

Overcoming Common Sales Obstacles

As a sales professional, you attempted all you could to accomplish your sales targets, such as working longer hours to close a transaction, working on weekends to see prospects at their convenience, and giving up sleep to follow up with prospects in other time zones. Despite your tireless efforts and unending sacrifices, you received only unanswered calls, disregarded emails, and unfavorable comments. You are not alone; most sales people are trapped in a never-ending cycle of disappointment. Sales representatives face several challenges on their path to success, stifling their progress. However, they tend to dismiss the issues that sum up to the eventual letdown. The only issue we have is that we believe we are not meant to have difficulties! Problems summon us to a higher level; confront and resolve them today. Potential difficulties are potential solutions. Below are common practical challenges likely to be faced in sales and preferred ways to tackle them:

When competing with lower-cost competitors, the most typical selling tactic employed by competitors to flourish in the market is to decrease their prices. Beating low-ballers may appear challenging for sales experts, but it is not impossible.

Solution

"Identify areas where you may compete favorably and create a comparison table." Be clear, and presume that your clients are aware of your competition. Some clients don't mind spending if they get good value for their money. So, use case studies, white papers, and client testimonials to demonstrate the value of your product. Educate your potential clients about the product's quality and benefits through seminars, demonstrations, and blogs. Determine and communicate your USP (unique selling proposition) to prospects.

Prospects cease replying, most sales professionals see a decline in response rate after the first few encounters. At this point, sales professionals can either dismiss the transaction or waste time trying to figure out why the prospect isn't responding.

Solution

A captivating subject line will pique their interest. Engage in a chat with another employee in that organization. Explore various contact hours. Call or contact your prospect at different timings in the day.

A lengthy sales cycle
When a deal is stalled in the pipeline for an extended period, it has a lower possibility of being converted into a sale. As a result, it is one of the key worries for sales representatives since it influences their conversion ratio.

Solution

Create an effective selling proposal.
Increase your contact rate.
Examine pipeline agreements regularly. Timely follow-up.
Boost prospect engagement.
Keep track of your sales figures.

There is no ability to connect with decision-makers. Sales representatives are unable to avoid the gatekeepers to pitch their solution to high-level decision makers with purchasing power. According to one study, 60% of a salesperson's time is spent in front of customers who are unwilling or unable to purchase their product or service.

Solution

Don't quit, also be confident in your ability to communicate with the person who has the ultimate say. Explain the advantages of including the decision-maker in the conversation. Impress the decision maker, his firm, and its operational challenges at the initial encounter.

Increasing Referrals and Repeat Sales

Referrals and repeat business are essential for long-term sales success. It's important we look at ways to generate recommendations from delighted customers and encourage repeat business through continuous relationship management. Improve on learning how to build a network of supporters that not only promote your products or services but also bring in new customers. Increasing referral sales is done easier by utilizing already existing connections to reach your sales target. This can be said to be a process of converting your relationships into income and keeping your consumers engaged and loyal.

Key idea 4

Modern Sales Tools and Techniques

Closing the deal

Staying ahead of the curve in the ever-changing world of sales necessitates a thorough awareness of the tools and strategies used by current sales professionals. This is your key to unlocking the techniques and technology that will boost your relationship-selling efforts.

Using Technology to Improve Relationship Building.

The most successful salespeople focus on larger, better, quicker, cheaper, and more profitable methods to market. They regard these sales methods as the key to continuous development and success, but there are only so many hours in the day. Fortunately, technological advancements are making it easier to utilize production capabilities and enhance performance. Programs, applications, and other tools enable sales agents to grow their companies in previously inconceivable ways. To take advantage of these possibilities, remember that the most valuable moment in the sales process is when you're in front of a client or prospect. Time spent on administrative and operational tasks is often necessary, but it is not the activity that generates the most value.

Here are three strategies to help you make the most of your time in front of buyers:

- Marketing automation, You must attract more individuals to get in front of them. Rocket referrals for example, assist agents in automatically harvesting recommendations and automating the posting of evaluations on social media. Others, such as HubSpot, may be used to plan and post across all social media channels, saving time and allowing marketing activities to occur outside of peak selling hours. With set-it-and-forget-it contact campaigns, HubSpot, Salesforce, Microsoft Dynamics, and other customer relationship management (CRM) solutions may also automate prospect-nurturing campaigns.

- Planning, tools like Calendly enable prospects and customers to arrange time with you at their leisure, boosting the chance of a meeting and that crucial face time. Scheduling solutions are most successful when paired with strong social media marketing and CRM "conveyor belts," which should try to direct prospects directly to your calendar.

- Tools that replicate you. Using video sales proposals is a simple approach to selling when you're away from the office—or even while you're sleeping. Video helps you save time on travel and scheduling while also recording several tailored pitches when you're at your best. Furthermore, it enables prospects to zero down on what is most important to them.

You may accomplish this effectively and convincingly with only your mobile phone, or you can take the method to the next level with video tools like Forge3. In addition, building your own YouTube channel allows you to enlighten, educate, and convince people 24 hours a day, seven days a week, and is a terrific addition to your automated marketing suite. There are several technological tools available to help you improve your performance and expand on your salesmanship. Some are new and specialized, while others are as common as your agency management system. The key to leveraging on the tools, magnifying and optimizing your selling time, is to use them. Begin small and see how your sales improve.

A Strategic Approach to Social Media and Sales

Social media has evolved into an essential component of current sales strategy. Every day, we witness the aggressive and smart use of social media in relationship selling. The good and bad influence of social media on businesses is enormous. Do you concur? This is supported by 90% of businesses. Whether you are a startup, a small business, an online store, or a large corporation, social media is critical to your business marketing plan. A survey shows that 71% of consumers who had a positive social media service experience with a business are inclined to suggest it to others. It demonstrates the significance of social media for businesses. Businesses should certainly use popular social media sites to stay competitive. Social media networks allow you to communicate with clients, raise brand recognition, and improve leads and sales. With over five billion people using social media worldwide, it's hardly a fleeting fad. Social media has significantly altered the corporate landscape. It is one of the most important parts of digital marketing, providing great advantages that enable a lot of customers world over to be reached. If you are a CEO or a small company owner, you must understand why you need to be on social media and how it will affect your business. Before you create your social media strategy, you should ask yourself many things. What are the methods via which my consumers can be found? How can I target my audience using such channels? What are my goals and the ROI of social media strategy? So it is clear how social media can have a significant impact on your business and be one of the most effective marketing platforms for reaching out to your target audience.

Key idea 5

Looking Forward

In the final stage of this book, relationship selling, we look ahead to see how the power of relationships will continue to affect the future of sales. As the company landscape changes and consumer expectations fluctuate, it is critical to plan for the future. We must align our viewpoints so that we can foresee the changes and possibilities that await us in the world of sales.

Relationship Selling in the Future

We have seen new trends and movements in the sales world. People's communication styles have evolved beyond social media and into the domain of relationship-centric marketing. Digital media has irrevocably altered the game, and firms must adapt to remain competitive. Businesses are learning that the same marketing methods they've used for years no longer work. People nowadays demand more than simply good products or services. They want deeper ties with the companies and businesses around them, not just a quick transaction. Conventional marketing methods are no longer effective. Companies must adjust their thinking and shift from transactional marketing to relationship marketing to win today. This is the only way they will be able to connect with people on a deeper level, build their business, and boost income. We are now in the relationship era, and firms must change swiftly to remain relevant. But how do you achieve this? How can you make the transition from transactional to relationship-centric marketing? What actions can you take to ensure your success? Where do you even begin? Let us now discuss relationship-centric marketing. People, in actuality, are no longer interested in being sold to. They are more interested in developing long-term relationships with individuals and businesses they like than in just making a single purchase. That is, in essence, what relationship-centric marketing is all about. It's all about developing more personal and meaningful ties with your consumers. It is opposed to transactional marketing. It all starts with building trust and a tight relationship with your consumers. You're not just going to say,

"Hey, I have this terrific stuff, here's the link, it'll be great for you!" Before everything else, you endeavor to understand your consumer. What are their issues? What do they require assistance with? You must make an effort to have a better knowledge of what you can give them and how you can assist them. This is the point at which the change begins. Relationship-centric marketing necessitates being more human than ever before, which is why it works so effectively. People like transparent businesses and want to be a part of your journey. They don't just want you to sell them anything. They want you to be a buddy they can rely on. This is why relationship-centric marketing works so well: it does not make consumers feel like they are being marketed to. It feels more personal, which is what consumers like.

Keeping Ahead in a Changing Sales Landscape

Sales professionals have the onerous burden of navigating a continually developing sales landscape in today's dynamic and fast-paced corporate climate. As client expectations vary rapidly, sales methods must adapt to maintain relevance and success. This book discusses the need to adjust to shifting consumer expectations and provides practical tips for successfully navigating this changing sales landscape. Because of technology improvements, shifting demographics, and changing market dynamics, the sales environment is undergoing substantial alterations. Customers are more aware and empowered than ever before, due to the wealth of information at their disposal. As a result, their expectations have shifted, and consumers now want personalized experiences, rapid replies, and smooth interactions across the sales process. Businesses must adapt to shifting client expectations to succeed in the developing sales market. Consider the following major strategies:

- Adopt a Customer-First Approach: A customer-centric strategy centers all sales activity on the customer. Understanding their requirements, preferences, and pain spots allows you to personalize the sales process accordingly. Businesses may improve customer happiness and loyalty by concentrating on creating relationships and providing tailored experiences.

- Utilize Data and Analytics: Data-driven insights are critical for understanding consumer behavior and preferences. Businesses may obtain important insights into consumer trends, uncover patterns, and make data-driven choices by employing analytics technologies. This data may be utilized to tailor sales techniques and give appropriate solutions to clients' changing needs.

- Improve the Sales Experience: Customers today demand seamless and frictionless interactions throughout the sales process. This involves providing user-friendly websites, mobile responsiveness, and effective communication channels. Businesses may improve the whole sales experience and gain a competitive advantage by investing in user-friendly technologies and efficient procedures.

- Build Strong Relationships: In the ever-changing sales world, it is critical to cultivate strong ties with customers. Establishing trust, providing outstanding customer service, and maintaining open channels of communication are critical for cultivating long-term relationships. Consistent follow-ups, individualized advice, and proactive issue resolution all demonstrate a commitment to client satisfaction.

- Continuous Learning and Adaptation: In a continuously changing sales world, being current on the newest trends, technology, and client expectations is critical. To improve their abilities and react to changing market circumstances, sales professionals should engage in ongoing learning and development. It is critical to embrace change and be nimble to stay ahead in the sales game.

Sales personnels must be proactive, nimble, and eager to embrace change to prosper in today's corporate climate. Businesses may position themselves for long-term success by remaining attentive to consumer demands, changing sales methods, and embracing technology. Remember that in the fast-paced world of sales, adapting is essential. Businesses that are adaptable and responsive will have a competitive edge as client expectations continue to grow. Organizations may stimulate development, increase customer happiness, and maintain their market position by navigating the dynamic sales landscape.

Conclusion

It's important we pay more attention to learning everything there is to know about relationship selling, including why it is still a crucial approach to master. As the world of sales continues to develop and evolve, so do the number of sales methods and tools available to assist teams in closing on new clients and retaining existing ones. Many of the old-school sales strategies don't always work anymore. It's a difficult environment for salesmen, particularly in business to business. However, there is a lot of expertise and approaches available to assist sales teams in achieving success and meeting their objectives. While the internet and hundreds of sales gurus all stating various things might make it easy to become overwhelmed with knowledge, there is one sales approach that every salesperson should master: relationship selling. Relationship selling has been around for a long time, but even in this digital era with advancements in sales tools, it still remains a crucial approach to grasp. But it makes sense; cultivating great working connections is essential for completing a new contract, maintaining current clients over time, and developing trust that may lead to new recommendations. While the relationship selling process appears to be quite easy, many sales teams overlook the fundamentals and the significance of caring more about the people than the product. This book should be useful whether you are new to the subject or just need a refresher. Understanding the buyer's perspective, determining their pain point, and then providing a solution is the relationship-selling method. To do it properly, the salesperson does not need to be a friend to the customer, but they must acquire the buyer's confidence and trust.